Quotations

on

Love

Compiled by Rosalie Maggio

BARNES
&NOBLE
BOOKS
NEW YORK

Till I loved I never lived.

EMILY DICKINSON

To David

$\mathcal{C}$ONTENTS

$\mathscr{I}$NTRODUCTION

In this collection of quotations, women and men confide their thoughts and feelings, their bewilderments and joys, about what we call romantic love. Although, like most people, I can name the heroic romances of history and literature, I am more deeply moved by the all-too-human loves at whose fires I've warmed my heart—those joyous, unpredictable, and lifegiving relationships that survive not only the slings and arrows of outrageous fortune but the stings and fleeting losses of everyday life.

Because many of our ideas of love come from its unrealistic portrayal in the mass culture, it is difficult to recognize the real thing. Certainly that breathless state compounded of hope, longing, and ecstasy is a form of love; it's just that we seem to have mistaken it for the *only* form of love.

I come closest to understanding love when I see it in people I know: those wildly mismatched couples who underwrite their commitment with daring leaps of faith; couples who build worlds of their own and then invite the rest of us in; those who remain faithful in body and spirit to each other through the death of a child, AIDS, bankruptcy, alcoholism, or chronic illness; the couples who must not only find their own internal harmonies but must struggle against prejudice because they do not meet arbitrary standards of "rightness."

Rarely has there been anything "typical" about the couples whose company I most enjoy: Sheri and Joe live half a continent apart, but you can't be five minutes in their company (when he goes there or she comes here) without feeling their closeness. Ed and Norman's love spills over to their daughter Maddy as well as to the hundreds of children enrolled in their Montessori schools. Armele and François as well as Judy and Don married each other in good health; they stayed married and in love when poor health for one of them arrived much too soon. Maggie and Deborah's love takes in an ever-widening circle of artists, musicians, family, and friends. Nick and David have stayed together so long, they say, because neither really understands the other. Terry and Paul have professional lives, three children, a twenty-year-old marriage, and the loving relationship we all wanted to have when we grew up.

Love's face isn't always smiling. A friend who had a remarkably loving and stable relationship once softly confessed to me in her careful Dutch accent, "Oh, my, the hate I have in my heart for that man." They had been trying to hang wallpaper together.

In one particularly luminous relationship, two soulmates didn't find each other until they were past fifty and they had only four years together before death took one of them. And even so, the love goes on; death can only do so much.

I hope some of these quotations will be read by two people to each other as they sit in front of a fireplace or at the edge of a lake or near a sleeping child or a sinkful of dishes. In the talk that follows they will learn at least one astonishing thing about the other person.

This book is dedicated to the tall blond stranger I've been sharing a home, checking account, love, towels, dinners, children, and ideas with for nearly thirty years. It's difficult to be sure, but I think it's love.

ove

Everyone admits that love is wonderful and necessary, yet no one can agree on what it is.

DIANE ACKERMAN

That love is all there is,
Is all we know of Love.

EMILY DICKINSON

love is the whole and more than all

E.E. CUMMINGS

Love alone matters.

ST. THÉRÈSE OF LISIEUX

Love is the white light of emotion.

DIANE ACKERMAN

Love is the light that you see by.

BESS STREETER ALDRICH

Love is the poetry of the senses.

HONORÉ DE BALZAC

Love is the wine of existence.

HENRY WARD BEECHER

Love is a game that two can play and both win.

EVA GABOR

Love in your heart wasn't put there to stay.
Love isn't love till you give it away.

OSCAR HAMMERSTEIN

The only love we keep is the love we give away.

ELBERT HUBBARD

Since love is not a thing, it is not lost when given.
You can offer your love completely to hundreds of
people and still retain the same love you had origi-
nally. It is like knowledge. The wise man can teach
all he knows and when he's through he'll still know
all that he has taught.

LEO BUSCAGLIA

Love has nothing to do with what you are expecting to get — only with what you are expecting to give — which is everything.

KATHARINE HEPBURN

Love consists in this, that two solitudes protect and touch and greet each other.

RAINER MARIA RILKE

Life has taught us that love does not consist in gazing at each other but in looking outward together in the same direction.

ANTOINE DE SAINT-EXUPÉRY

Love is the extremely difficult realization that something other than oneself is real.

IRIS MURDOCH

Love is that condition in which the happiness of another person is essential to your own.

ROBERT A. HEINLEIN

Love is the strange bewilderment which overtakes one person on account of another person.

JAMES THURBER AND E.B. WHITE

Love is friendship set on fire.

JEREMY TAYLOR

Love is, above all, the gift of oneself.

JEAN ANOUILH

In the capacities of loving, as in all other capacities, there be diversities of gifts.

C.M. SEDGWICK

Love, first begotten of all created things.

GEORGIANA GODDARD KING

For love is heaven, and heaven is love.

WALTER SCOTT

Love is the only gold.

ALFRED, LORD TENNYSON

Where there is great love, there are always miracles.

WILLA CATHER

In for a penny, in for a pound—
It's Love that makes the world go round!

W.S. GILBERT

Love doesn't make the world go round. Love is what makes the ride worthwhile.

FRANKLIN P. JONES

Love doesn't really make the world go round. It just makes people dizzy so it looks like it.

MARTHA LUPTON

Love is the magician, the enchanter, that changes worthless things to joy, and makes right royal kings and queens of common clay. It is the perfume of that wondrous flower, the heart, and without that sacred passion, that divine swoon, we are less than beasts; but with it, earth is heaven, and we are gods.

ROBERT G. INGERSOLL

Love is a fruit in season at all times.

MOTHER TERESA

Love — is anterior to life —
Posterior — to death.

EMILY DICKINSON

One word frees us of all the weight and pain of life: That word is love.

SOPHOCLES

There is a land of the living and a land of the dead and the bridge is love, the only survival, the only meaning.

THORNTON WILDER

Love spends his all, and still hath store.

PHILIP JAMES BAILEY

Love much. Earth has enough of bitter in it.

ELLA WHEELER WILCOX

We love because it's the only true adventure.

NIKKI GIOVANNI

Love is intensity, that second in which the doors of time and space open just a crack.

OCTAVIO PAZ

Whoever has loved knows all that life contains of sorrow and of joy.

GEORGE SAND

A great love is an absolute isolation and an absolute absorption.

OUIDA

It was a great holiness, a religion, as all great loves must be.

ELSIE DE WOLFE

Love is the most universal, formidable and mysterious of cosmic energies.

TEILHARD DE CHARDIN

Love is the most terrible, and also the most generous, of the passions; it is the only one which includes in its dreams the happiness of someone else.

ALPHONSE KARR

Love is an attempt to change a piece of a dreamworld into reality.

THEODOR REIK

Love is always in the mood of believing in miracles.

JOHN COWPER POWYS

Love is the key to the solution of the problems of the world.

MARTIN LUTHER KING, JR.

The beginning of my history is—love. It is the beginning of every man and every woman's history, if they are only frank enough to admit it.

MARIE CORELLI

There is only one happiness in life, to love and be loved.

GEORGE SAND

The greatest happiness of life is the conviction that we are loved.

VICTOR HUGO

That we all desire to be desired by one we desire is the one uncontested human proposition.

SEBASTIAN MOORE

Love is an irresistible desire to be irresistibly desired.

ROBERT FROST

Every heart desires a mate.

MARIE STOPES

Romantic love is not a myth, waiting to be discarded, but, for most of us, a discovery, waiting to be born.

NATHANIEL BRANDEN

To love is to choose.

JOSEPH ROUX

Love is the true price of love.

GEORGE HERBERT

Love is the only thing that keeps me sane.

SUE TOWNSEND

Love is the only sane and satisfactory answer to the problem of human existence.

ERICH FROMM

The sanest thing in this world is love.

ANNE SEXTON

Many a man does not find his heart until he has lost his head.

FRIEDRICH NIETZSCHE

Love is like an hourglass, with the heart filling up as the brain empties.

JULES RENARD

Oh, the comfort—the inexpressible comfort of feeling *safe* with a person—having neither to weigh thoughts nor measure words, but pouring them all right out, just as they are, chaff and grain together; certain that a faithful hand will take and sift them, keep what is worth keeping, and then with the breath of kindness blow the rest away.

DINAH MARIA MULOCK CRAIK

Love is an act of faith, and whoever is of little faith is also of little love.

ERIC FROMM

To be in love is to surpass oneself.

OSCAR WILDE

Love is the falling rain,
Love is the following flood,
And love is the ark
With two of a kind aboard.

BARBARA DEMING

Love is merely passion with a holy name.

OSCAR WILDE

Love is the same as like except you feel sexier.

JUDITH VIORST

Whoso loves
Believes the impossible.

ELIZABETH BARRETT BROWNING

True love is but a humble, low born thing.
And hath its food served up in earthenware;
It is a thing to walk with, hand in hand,
Through the every-dayness of this workday world.

JAMES RUSSELL LOWELL

But true love is a durable fire,
In the mind ever burning,
Never sick, never old, never dead,
From itself never turning.

WALTER RALEIGH

O tell her, brief is life but love is long.

ALFRED, LORD TENNYSON

Love decreases when it ceases to increase.

FRANÇOIS RENÉ DE CHATEAUBRIAND

Love doesn't just sit there, like a stone, it has to be made, like bread; re-made all the time, made new.

URSULA K. LE GUIN

Love is never complete in any person. There is
always room for growth.

LEO BUSCAGLIA

Where love is concerned, too much is not even
enough.

PIERRE DE BEAUMARCHAIS

It was a love like a chord from Bach,
of such pure gravity.

NINA CASSIAN

Love possesses not nor would it be possessed;
For love is sufficient unto love.

KAHLIL GIBRAN

Love is always open arms. If you close your arms about love you will find that you are left holding only yourself.

LEO BUSCAGLIA

Love is like quicksilver in the hand. Leave the fingers open and it stays. Clutch it, and it darts away.

DOROTHY PARKER

Love will not always linger longest
With those who hold it in too clenched a fist.

ALICE DUER MILLER

We cannot possess love, only be possessed by it.

STEPHEN AND ONDREA LEVINE

Love—that arbitrary and inexorable tyrant.

HARRIET E. WILSON

Love is a dangerous angel. . . . Especially nowadays.

FRANCESCA LIA BLOCK

Love is the wild card of existence.

RITA MAE BROWN

Her loves were so varied that no rule could be discovered by which to judge them. She loved wildly, without either chart or compass . . . a thing of torn sails and stricken masts, that never came within sight of a harbor.

RADCLYFFE HALL

Love was a great disturbance.

NAOMI ROYDE-SMITH

One hour of right-down love
Is worth an age of dully living on.

APHRA BEHN

We have all known the long loneliness and we have learned that the only solution is love.

DOROTHY DAY

People who are sensible about love are incapable of it.

DOUGLAS YATES

Of all the forms of caution, caution in love is perhaps the most fatal to true happiness.

BERTRAND RUSSELL

Before we love with our heart, we already love with our imagination.

LOUISE COLET

Love is purely a creation of the human imagination . . . perhaps the most important of all the examples of how the imagination continually outruns the creature it inhabits.

KATHERINE ANNE PORTER

When love comes it comes without effort, like perfect weather.

HELEN YGLESIAS

Love cannot be forced, love cannot be coaxed and teased. It comes out of Heaven, unasked and unsought.

PEARL S. BUCK

If it is your time love will track you like a cruise missile. If you say "No! I don't want it right now," that's when you'll get it for sure. Love will make a way out of no way. Love is an exploding cigar which we willingly smoke.

LYNDA BARRY

Love might have consoled him by taking him by surprise; for that is the only way in which love does console. One cannot find it when one seeks it; it comes to us when we do not expect it.

GEORGE SAND

There is no disguise which can for long conceal love where it exists or simulate it where it does not.

FRANÇOIS DE LA ROCHEFOUCAULD

We receive love . . . not in proportion to our demands or sacrifices or needs, but roughly in proportion to our own capacity to love.

ROLLO MAY

The simple but observable fact is that the more you love, the more you are able to love.

JOYCE BROTHERS

For one human being to love another human being: that is perhaps the most difficult task that has been entrusted to us, the ultimate task, the final test and proof, the work for which all other work is merely preparation.

RAINER MARIA RILKE

To be capable of giving and receiving mature love is as sound a criterion as we have for the fulfilled personality. But by that very token it is a goal gained only in proportion to how much one has fulfilled the prior condition of becoming a person in one's own right.

ROLLO MAY

When souls really touch, it is forever. Then space and time disappear, and all that remains is the consciousness that we are not alone in life.

JOAN CHITTISTER

We are all born for love. . . . It is the principle of existence and its only end.

BENJAMIN DISRAELI

Love is repaid by love alone.

ST. THÉRÈSE OF LISIEUX

If one is out of touch with oneself, then one cannot touch others.

ANNE MORROW LINDBERGH

The most enlightened prayer isn't "Dear God, send me someone wonderful," but, "Dear God, help me realize that I am someone wonderful."

MARIANNE WILLIAMSON

Till it has loved, no man or woman can become itself.

EMILY DICKINSON

Until we love, we really do not even know who we are.

RICHARD ROHR

Perhaps loving something is the only starting place there is for making your life your own.

ALICE KOLLER

To love means to commit oneself without guarantee, to give oneself completely in the hope that our love will produce love in the loved person.

ERICH FROMM

Love goes toward love.

WILLIAM SHAKESPEARE

Love begets love. This torment is my joy.

THEODORE ROETHKE

We never live so intensely as when we love strongly. We never realize ourselves so vividly as when we are in the full glow of love for others.

WALTER RAUSCHENBUSCH

Perhaps it does not matter so very much what it is one loves in this world. But love something one must.

KATHERINE MANSFIELD

There are as many kinds of loves as there are flowers: everlastings that never wither; speedwells that wait for the wind to fan them out of life; blood-red mountain-lilies that pour their voluptuous sweetness out for one day, and lie in the dust at night. There is no one flower has the charm of all.

RALPH IRON

There are people whom one loves immediately and for ever. Even to know they are alive in the world with one is quite enough.

NANCY SPAIN

If you have love in your life it can make up for a great many things that are missing. If you don't have love in your life, no matter what else there is, it's not enough.

ANN LANDERS

Till I loved
I never lived—enough.

EMILY DICKINSON

Love, then, hath every bliss in store;
'Tis friendship, and 'tis something more.
Each other every wish they give;
Not to know love is not to live.

JOHN GAY

Love has the quality of informing almost everything—
even one's work.

SYLVIA ASHTON-WARNER

When you send out real love, real love will return
to you.

FLORENCE SCOVEL SHINN

The absolute yearning of one human body for another particular one and its indifference to substitutes is one of life's major mysteries.

IRIS MURDOCH

When the desire is on for one particular person, nobody else will do.

CAITLIN THOMAS

Who ever loved that loved not at first sight?

CHRISTOPHER MARLOWE

I saw and loved.

EDWARD GIBBON

O, there is nothing holier, in this life of ours, than the first consciousness of love,—the first fluttering of its silken wings.

HENRY WADSWORTH LONGFELLOW

To see coming toward you the face that will mean an end of oneness is—far more than birth itself—the beginning of life.

HOLLY ROTH

Love is in constant potential and sometimes the mind is the last to know. But the heart may sense from across the room, from across worlds, that the beloved is approaching and the journey of another lifetime is about to begin.

STEPHEN AND ONDREA LEVINE

It is difficult to know at what moment love begins; it is less difficult to know that it has begun.

HENRY WADSWORTH LONGFELLOW

I only met him by accident. No, I don't know why I said that. I guess you meet everyone by accident.

KATHLEEN WINSOR

The story of a love is not important—what is important is that one is capable of love. It is perhaps the only glimpse we are permitted of eternity.

HELEN HAYES

We love as soon as we learn to distinguish a separate "you" and "me." Love is our attempt to assuage the terror and isolation of that separateness.

JUDITH VIORST

You can love only in proportion to your capacity for independence.

ROLLO MAY

We need more than love to make love last.

NATHANIEL BRANDEN AND E. DEVERS BRANDEN

The emotions of love, in spite of the romantics, is not self-sustaining; it endures only when the lovers love many things together, and not merely each other.

WALTER LIPPMANN

Love opens the doors into everything, as far as I can see, including and perhaps most of all, the door into one's own secret, and often terrible and frightening, real self.

MAY SARTON

Love is the vital essence that pervades and permeates, from the center to the circumference, the graduating circles of all thought and action. Love is the talisman of human weal and woe—the open sesame to every soul.

ELIZABETH CADY STANTON

The sweetest joy, the wildest woe is love.

PHILIP JAMES BAILEY

Love is most nearly itself
When here and now cease to matter.

T.S. ELIOT

Love is content with the present, it hopes for the future, and it doesn't brood over the past.

ANN LANDERS

In a great romance, each person basically plays a part that the other really likes.

ELIZABETH ASHLEY

The fate of love is, that it always sees too little or too much.

AMELIA E. BARR

Romantic love has always seemed to me unaccountable, unassailable, unforgettable, and nearly always unattainable.

MARGARET ANDERSON

Secretly, we wish anyone we love will think exactly the way we do.

KIM CHERNIN

We hide the truer part of ourselves when we love.

EDNA O'BRIEN

Each one of us thinks our experience of love is different from everybody else's.

VIBHAVARI SHIRURKAR

While it is a misfortune to a woman never to be loved, it is a tragedy to her never to love.

DOROTHY DIX

It is the loving, not the loved, woman who feels lovable.

JESSAMYN WEST

Most of us love from our need to love not
because we find someone deserving.

NIKKI GIOVANNI

Too many times we insist on loving people the way
we want to love them instead of the way they need
to be loved.

JOAN CHITTISTER

The hardest-learned lesson: that people have only
their kind of love to give, not our kind.

MIGNON MCLAUGHLIN

The more you love someone the more he wants
from you and the less you have to give since you've
already given him your love.

NIKKI GIOVANNI

I'd always rather be with people who loved me too little rather than with people who loved me too much.

KATHERINE MANSFIELD

Being always overavid, I demand from those I love a love equal to mine, which, being balanced people, they cannot supply.

SYLVIA ASHTON-WARNER

I will never love, for I should never be loved as I desire to be loved.

MARIE BASHKIRTSEFF

I think I'm a love agnostic—not sure, one way or another, if it really exists.

JOAN M. DRURY

To cheat oneself out of love is the most terrible deception; it is an eternal loss for which there is no reparation, either in time or in eternity.

SÖREN KIERKEGAARD

No one has ever loved anyone the way everyone wants to be loved.

MIGNON MCLAUGHLIN

Love never dies of starvation, but often of indigestion.

NINON DE LENCLOS

You need somebody to love you while you're looking for someone to love.

SHELAGH DELANEY

Clea was a woman who adored love. Hormones had always been her recreational drug of choice.

LISA ALTHER

Love is a state of mind that begins when you think life can't be any better, and ends when you think life can't be any worse.

ANONYMOUS

Love requires peace, love will dream; it cannot live upon the remnants of our time and our personality.

ELLEN KEY

Love cannot survive if you just give it scraps of yourself, scraps of your time, scraps of your thoughts.

MARY O'HARA

We only deliberately waste time with those we love—it is the purest sign that we love someone if we choose to spend time idly in their presence when we could be doing something more "constructive."

SHEILA CASSIDY

Falling in love is a matter of intermittent propinquity. The cure is—propinquity.

ELBERT HUBBARD

True love isn't the kind that endures through long years of absence, but the kind that endures through long years of propinquity.

HELEN ROWLAND

We must resemble each other a little in order to understand each other, but we must be a little different to love each other.

PAUL GÉRALDY

It is impossible to love and be wise.

FRANCIS BACON

Love is the wisdom of the fool and the folly of the wise.

SAMUEL JOHNSON

We love what we should scorn if we were wiser.

MARIE DE FRANCE

Love says, mine. Love says, I could eat you up. Love
says, stay as you are, be my own private thing, don't
you dare have ideas I don't share. Love has just got
to gobble the other, bones and all, crunch. I don't
want to do that. I sure don't want it done to me!

MARGE PIERCY

Perhaps that is what love is—the momentary or
prolonged refusal to think of another person in
terms of power.

PHYLLIS ROSE

I dream that love without tyranny is possible.

ANDREA DWORKIN

Where love rules, there is no will to power; and where power predominates, there love is lacking. The one is the shadow of the other.

C.G. JUNG

Love is the child of freedom, never that of domination.

ERICH FROMM

Shall I tell you what makes love so dangerous? 'Tis the too high idea we are apt to form of it.

NINON DE LENCLOS

Because it corresponds to a vital need, love is over-valued in our culture. It becomes a phantom—like success—carrying with it the illusion that it is a solution for all problems.

KAREN HORNEY

Learning to love will proceed most soundly if we cease trying to persuade ourselves that to love is easy, and if we are realistic enough to abandon the illusory masquerades for love in a society which is always talking about love but has so little of it.

ROLLO MAY

The course of true love never did run smooth.

SHAKESPEARE

True love is like a ghost; everyone talks of it, but few have met it face to face.

FRANÇOIS DE LA ROCHEFOUCAULD

If only one could tell true love from false love as one can tell mushrooms from toadstools.

KATHERINE MANSFIELD

Love is a choice—not simply, or necessarily, a rational choice, but rather a willingness to be present to others without pretense or guile.

CARTER HEYWARD

Love conquers all things; let us too surrender to Love.

VIRGIL

She did observe, with some dismay, that, far from conquering all, love lazily sidestepped practical problems.

JEAN STAFFORD

Whoever said love conquers all was a fool. Because almost everything conquers love—or tries to.

EDNA FERBER

I am not sure at all
if love is salve
or just
a deeper kind of wound.
I do not think it matters.

ERICA JONG

The pain of love is the pain of being alive. It's a per-
petual wound.

MAUREEN DUFFY

Mortal love is but the licking of honey from thorns.

ANONYMOUS

Intense love is often akin to intense suffering.

FRANCES ELLEN WATKINS HARPER

The truth is simple:
you do not die
from love.
You only wish
you did.

ERICA JONG

Love all the people you can. The sufferings
from love are not to be compared to the sorrows
of loneliness.

SUSAN HALE

The love that lasts the longest is the love that is
never returned.

W. SOMERSET MAUGHAM

To care passionately for another human creature brings always more sorrow than joy; but all the same . . . one would not be without that experience.

AGATHA CHRISTIE

I wonder why love is so often equated with joy when it is everything else as well. Devastation, balm, obsession, granting and receiving excessive value, and losing it again. It is recognition, often of what you are not but might be. It sears and it heals. It is beyond pity and above law. It can seem like truth.

FLORIDA SCOTT-MAXWELL

What we have once enjoyed we can never lose. All that we love deeply becomes a part of us.

HELEN KELLER

Never doubt love. . . Never question it when it comes onstage, but be happy for its entrance. And do not weep when it makes its exit, for it leaves behind it the sweet aroma of caring, a fragrance to linger the rest of your life.

HELEN VAN SLYKE

It is impossible to repent of love. The sin of love does not exist.

MURIEL SPARK

'Tis better to have loved and lost
Than never to have loved at all.

ALFRED, LORD TENNYSON

Love, like poetry, is a kind of homesickness,
the kind which made medieval monks
sleep in their coffins.

JENNIFER STONE

The night was dark
and love was a burning fence
about my house.

AUDRE LORDE

Soft are the hands of Love,
soft, soft are his feet.

H.D.

To be in love
Is to touch things with a lighter hand.

GWENDOLYN BROOKS

I always want to be in love, always. It's like being a
tuning fork.

EDNA O'BRIEN

I must have true love or nothing.

JULIETTE DROUET

To live without loving is not really to live.

MOLIÈRE

I don't want to live—I want to love first, and live incidentally.

ZELDA FITZGERALD

The final word is love.

DOROTHY DAY

overs

Lovers re-create the world.

CARTER HEYWARD

Two souls with but a single thought,
Two hearts that beat as one.

MARIA LOVELL

Two minds without a single thought.

PHILIP BARRY

Every love affair is a private universe.

NATHANIEL BRANDEN AND E. DEVERS BRANDEN

All really great lovers are articulate, and verbal seduction is the surest road to actual seduction.

MARYA MANNES

Anyone can be passionate, but it takes real lovers to be silly.

ROSE FRANKEN

Two persons love in one another the future good which they aid one another to unfold.

MARGARET FULLER

Love, genuine love, makes people good.

VICTORIA WOLFF

Each will have two lives, a doubled state;
Each in himself will live, and in his mate.

LOUISE LABÉ

Let no one who loves be called altogether unhappy.

JAMES MATTHEW BARRIE

The great pairs of lovers in history only became the great pairs of lovers in history because they never got each other.

ANONYMOUS

The love that passeth all understanding is in the movies.

MARTHA LUPTON

Lovers should guard their strangeness.

RALPH WALDO EMERSON

It is just as hard to live with the person we love as to love the person we live with.

JEAN ROSTAND

Love is banality to all outsiders.

MAE WEST

It is universally allowed that, though nothing can be more interesting in itself than the conversation of two lovers, yet nothing can be more insipid in detail—just as the heavenly fragrance of the rose becomes vapid and sickly under all the attempts made to retain and embody its exquisite odor.

SUSAN FERRIER

People in love, it is well known, suffer extreme conceptual delusions; the most common of these being that other people find your condition as thrilling and eye-watering as you do yourselves.

JULIAN BARNES

The next greatest pleasure to love is to talk of love.

LOUISE LABÉ

To speak of love is to make love.

HONORÉ DE BALZAC

I like not only to be loved, but also to be told that I am loved. I am not sure that you are of the same mind. But the realm of silence is large enough beyond the grave. This is the world of light and speech, and I shall take leave to tell you that you are very dear.

GEORGE ELIOT

The lover and the physician are each popular from the same cause—we talk to them of nothing but ourselves.

L.E. Landon

All mankind love a lover.

Ralph Waldo Emerson

It is not so much true that all the world loves a lover as that a lover loves all the world.

Ruth Rendell

All the world loves a lover, but it usually runs away from him when he talks.

Frank Moore Colby

$\mathcal{H}$OW DO I LOVE THEE?

How do I love thee? Let me count the ways.
I love thee to the depth and breadth and height
My soul can reach.

ELIZABETH BARRETT BROWNING

I love you more than yesterday, less than tomorrow.

EDMOND ROSTAND

Each day I love you more,
Today more than yesterday and less than tomorrow.

ROSEMONDE GÉRARD

Come live with me, and be my love;
And we will all the pleasures prove.

CHRISTOPHER MARLOWE

Come live with me, and be my love,
And we will some new pleasures prove.

JOHN DONNE

A jug of wine, a loaf of bread—and thou.

EDWARD FITZGERALD

To see her is to love her,
Love but her, and love for ever.

ROBERT BURNS

I've looked around enough to know
That you're the one I want to go
Through time with.

JIM CROCE

I long to believe in immortality. . . . If I am destined
to be happy with you here—how short is the longest
life. I wish to believe in immortality—I wish to live
with you forever.

JOHN KEATS

Getting to know you meant the shock of relearning
how simple joy was. Walking with you in the morn-
ing, having wine together over a late dinner, trying to
hold back the time when we were together: delight
needed no stimulus; it had become our element.

MALCOLM BOYD

Unremembered and afar
I watched you as I watched a star,
Through darkness struggling into view
And I loved you better than you knew.

ELIZABETH AKERS ALLEN

How long I've loved thee, and how well—
I dare not tell!

MARGARET DELAND

If I love you, what business is it of yours?

JOHANN WOLFGANG VON GOETHE

I felt your love as a benediction
In tranquil branches above me spread,
Over my sometimes troubled head.

VITA SACKVILLE-WEST

We find rest in those we love, and we provide a
resting place in ourselves for those who love us.

ST. BERNARD OF CLAIRVAUX

My heart shall be thy garden.

ALICE MEYNELL

I am two fools, I know,
For loving, and for saying so
In whining poetry.

JOHN DONNE

O Love, how thou art tired out with rhyme!
Thou art a tree whereon all poets clime.

MARGARET CAVENDISH

At the touch of love, everyone becomes a poet.

PLATO

Love demands expression. It will not stay still, stay silent, be good, be modest, be seen and not heard, no. It will break out in tongues of praise, the high note that smashes the glass and spills the liquid.

JEANETTE WINTERSON

If you press me to say why I loved him, I can say no more than it was because he was he and I was I.

MICHEL EYQUEM DE MONTAIGNE

A human being loves another, because he is who and what he is; he seeks the other's own self; he seeks what makes the other this particular individual person. To love means to say: it is good that you are you, it is very good.

LADISLAUS BOROS

Love is the will to let those we love be perfectly themselves, the resolution not to twist them to fit our own image. If in loving them we do not love what they are, but only their potential likeness to ourselves, then we do not love them; we only love the reflection of ourselves we find in them.

THOMAS MERTON

They do not love that do not show their love.

WILLIAM SHAKESPEARE

A fire that no longer blazes is quickly smothered in ashes. Only a love that scorches and dazzles is worthy of the name. Mine is like that.

JULIETTE DROUET

Love is a fire. But whether it is going to warm your hearth or burn down your house, you can never tell.

JOAN CRAWFORD

I love you more than my own skin.

FRIDA KAHLO

I am my beloved's, and my beloved is mine.

THE SHULAMITE

Whatever our souls are made of, his and mine are
the same.

EMILY BRONTË

We never leave each other.
When does your mouth
say goodbye to your heart?

MARY TALLMOUNTAIN

If I had never met him I would have dreamed him
into being.

ANZIA YEZIERSKA

With each touch of you
i am fresh bread
warm and rising.

PAT PARKER

A woman I love
draws me a bath
of old roses.

AUDRE LORDE

He said he would love me like a revolution, like a
religion.

SANDRA CISNEROS

He gave her a look you could of poured on a waffle.

RING LARDNER

My love for you is more
Athletic than a verb.

SYLVIA PLATH

I see only you, think only of you, speak only to you, touch only you, breathe you, desire you, dream of you; in a word, I love you!

JULIETTE DROUET

My love for you's so strong
That no one could kill it—not even you.

ANNA AKHMATOVA

Ah! life grows lovely where you are.

MATHILDE BLIND

There is no question for which
you are not the answer.

BONNIE ZUCKER GOLDSMITH

No riches from his scanty store
My lover could impart;
He gave a boon I valued more—
He gave me all his heart!

HELEN MARIA WILLIAMS

Love—bittersweet, irrepressible—
loosens my limbs and I tremble.

SAPPHO

Love me in full being.

ELIZABETH BARRETT BROWNING

To love and be loved is to feel the sun from both
sides.

DAVID VISCOTT

I have drunk of the wine of life at last, I have known the thing best worth knowing, I have been warmed through and through, never to grow quite cold again till the end.

EDITH WHARTON

I love you *because* I love you, because it would be impossible for me not to love you. I love you without question, without calculation, without reason good or bad, faithfully, with all my heart and soul, and every faculty.

JULIETTE DROUET

I love you so passionately, that I hide a great part of my love, not to oppress you with it.

MARIE DE RABUTIN-CHANTAL

There is a stage with people we love when we are no longer separate from them, but so close in sympathy that we live through them as directly as through ourselves. . . . We push back our hair because theirs is in their eyes.

NAN FAIRBROTHER

There is a love that begins in the head, and goes down to the heart, and grows slowly; but it lasts till death, and asks less than it gives. There is another love, that blots out wisdom, that is sweet with the sweetness of life and bitter with the bitterness of death, lasting for an hour; but it is worth having lived a whole life for that hour.

RALPH IRON

Brevity may be the soul of wit, but not when someone's saying, "I love you."

JUDITH VIORST

Why is it that the most unoriginal thing we can say to one another is still the thing we long to hear? "I love you" is always a quotation.

JEANETTE WINTERSON

And what do all the great words come to in the end, but that?—I love you—I am at rest with you—I have come home.

DOROTHY L. SAYERS

He loves but little who
Can say and count in words, how much he loves.

DANTE ALIGHIERI

To be able to say how much you love is to love but little.

PETRARCH

Those that love the most speak least.

GEORGE PETTIE

The verb "to love" in Persian is "to have a friend." "I love you" translated literally is "I have you as a friend," and "I don't like you" simply means "I don't have you as a friend."

SHUSHA GUPPY

When I am dead, I am certain that the imprint of my love will be found on my heart. It is impossible to worship as I do without leaving some visible trace behind when life is over.

JULIETTE DROUET

I could dispense with life sooner than with your love.

JULIETTE DROUET

I love thee with a love I seemed to lose
With my lost saints,—I love thee with the breath,
Smiles, tears, of all my life!—and, if God choose,
I shall but love thee better after death.

ELIZABETH BARRETT BROWNING

*L*OVE LETTERS

There's no finer caress than a love letter, because it makes the world very small, and the writer and reader, the only rulers.

CECILIA CAPUZZI

Letters were first invented for consoling such solitary wretches as myself. Having lost the substantial pleasures of seeing and possessing you, I shall in some measure compensate this loss by the satisfaction I shall find in your writing.

HÉLOÏSE TO ABELARD

Our first love-letter . . . the dread of saying too much is so nicely balanced by the fear of saying too little. Hope borders on presumption, and fear on reproach.

L.E. LANDON

A love letter begins by your not knowing what you are going to say, and ends by your not knowing what you have said.

ANONYMOUS

It is the illusion of all lovers to think themselves unique and their words immortal.

HAN SUYIN

Beware of the man who writes flowery love letters;
he is preparing for years of silence.

ERICA JONG

I do not think that life has a suspense more sickening
than that of expecting a letter which does not come.

L.E. LANDON

A real love letter is absolutely ridiculous to everyone
except the writer and the recipient.

MYRTLE REED

All the world loves a lover, but it laughs when they
get hold of his love letters.

ANONYMOUS

INDING EACH OTHER

I flee who chases me, and chase who flees me.

OVID

The fickleness of the woman I love is only equaled by the infernal constancy of the women who love me.

GEORGE BERNARD SHAW

I never liked the men I loved, and never loved the men I liked.

FANNY BRICE

Seven years would be insufficient to make some people acquainted with each other, and seven days are more than enough for others.

JANE AUSTEN

The minute I heard my first love story
I started looking for you, not knowing . . .
Lovers don't finally meet somewhere.
They're in each other all along.

RUMI

People always remember the tune they fell in love to.

RUTH WOLFF

Getting to know someone, entering that new world,
is an ultimate, irretrievable leap into the unknown.
The prospect is terrifying. The stakes are high. The
emotions are overwhelming.

ELDRIDGE CLEAVER

It is easier to win love than to keep it.

DIANE DE POITIERS

It would be a happier world if love were as easy to keep as it is to make.

ANONYMOUS

Platonic friendship:—The interval between the introduction and the first kiss.

SOPHIE IRENE LOEB

It is lonely out here. We recognize each other. And, having recognized each other, is it any wonder that our souls hold hands and cling together even while our minds equivocate, hesitate, vacillate, and tremble?

ELDRIDGE CLEAVER

He drew a circle that shut me out—
Heretic, rebel, a thing to flout.
But Love and I had the wit to win:
We drew a circle that took him in!

EDWIN MARKHAM

I've got a heart like a college prom. Each one I
dance with seems the best of all.

ILKA CHASE

A girl can have two beaus to her string, can't she?

RICHARD SHATTUCK

If you never want to see a man again, say, "I love
you, I want to marry you, I want to have children"—
they leave skid marks.

RITA RUDNER

I waited
For the phone to ring
And when at last
It didn't,
I knew it was you.

ELEANOR BRON

When someone asks, "Why do you think he's not calling me?" there's always one answer—"He's not interested." There's not ever any other answer.

FRAN LEBOWITZ

There is no noise louder than a silent phone.

LOIS WYSE

My boyfriend and I broke up. He wanted to get married, and I didn't want him to.

RITA RUDNER

Love clamors far more incessantly and passionately at a closed gate than an open one!

MARIE CORELLI

The man she had was kind and clean
And well enough for every day,
But, oh, dear friends, you should have seen
The one that got away!

DOROTHY PARKER

The three most common myths of modern romance: 1. Single men would prefer being married. 2. Married men actually leave their wives. 3. Men who wear gold chains give gold rings.

LINDA SUNSHINE

The main reason to live with a man: You will never have to go on dates again.

STEPHANIE BRUSH

In Jacqueline's experience, charming out-of-the-way restaurants were frequently attached to out-of-the-way motels.

ELIZABETH PETERS

I have no-fail chemistry. A guy turns me on, he's the wrong one for me.

LINDA BARNES

A great many people fall in love with or feel attracted to a person who offers the least possibility of a harmonious union.

RUDOLF DREIKURS

I will not go out with a man who wears more jewelry than me, and I'll never, ever go to bed with a guy who calls me Babe. Other than that, however, I'm real flexible.

LINDA SUNSHINE

If you go to the grocery store wearing hair curlers and sweats, you'll run into the man of your dreams.

LISA COFIELD, DEBBIE DINGERSON, AND LEA RUSH

I've figured out why first dates don't work any better than they do. It's because they take place in restaurants. Women are weird and confused and unhappy about food, and men are weird and confused and unhappy about money, yet off they go, the minute they meet, to where you use money to buy food.

ADAIR LARA

There is too little courtship in the world. . . . For courtship means a wish to stand well in the other person's eyes, and, what is more, a readiness to be pleased with the other's ways; a sense on each side of having had the better of the bargain; an undercurrent of surprise and thankfulness at one's good luck.

VERNON LEE

Blessed is the wooing that is not long a-doing.

ROBERT BURTON

Flirtation is merely an expression of considered desire coupled with an admission of its impracticability.

MARYA MANNES

Flirtation . . . is a graceful salute to sex, a small impermanent spark between one human being and another, between a man and a woman not in need of fire.

MARYA MANNES

ISSES

Lord, I wonder what fool it was that first invented kissing!

JONATHAN SWIFT

A kiss can be a comma, a question mark or an exclamation point.

MISTINGUETTE

When you kiss me,
jaguars lope through my knees;
when you kiss me, my lips quiver like bronze
violets; oh, when you kiss me.

DIANE ACKERMAN

Her lips were so near
That—what else could I do?

WALTER LEARNED

His kissing is as full of sanctity as the touch of holy
bread.

WILLIAM SHAKESPEARE

Kissing was like death from lightning. If it hap-
pened, you didn't know it. And vice versa.

JESSAMYN WEST

A kiss is something which you cannot give without taking, and cannot take without giving.

ANONYMOUS

The kiss you take is paid by that you give:
The joy is mutual, and I'm still in debt.

GEORGE GRANVILLE

Ruby wasn't particular whom she kissed. In fact she led a regular mouth-to-mouth existence.

LILLIAN DAY

Some men kiss and do not tell, some kiss and tell;
but George Moore told and did not kiss.

SUSAN MITCHELL

$\mathcal{S}$ex

Touch is the meaning of being human.

ANDREA DWORKIN

Human thirsts are satisfied from time to time, but the thirst of the human skin is never satisfied so long as it lives.

JOYCE CAROL OATES

Truly, a little love-making is a very pleasant thing.

L.E. LANDON

Sex is an emotion in motion.

MAE WEST

Sex is a game, a weapon, a toy, a joy, a trance, an enlightenment, a loss, a hope.

SALLIE TISDALE

The human need for love and sex is made to bear the burden of all our bodily starvation for contact and sensation, all our creative starvation, all our need for social contact, and even our need to find meaning in our lives.

DEIRDRE ENGLISH AND BARBARA EHRENREICH

How little do they know human nature, who think they can say to passion, so far shalt thou go, and no farther!

SARAH SCOTT

How helpless we are, like netted birds, when we are caught by desire!

BELVA PLAIN

Love is the answer, but while you're waiting for the answer sex raises some pretty good questions.

WOODY ALLEN

Everyone lies about sex, more or less, to themselves if not to others, to others if not to themselves, exaggerating its importance or minimizing its pull.

DAPHNE MERKIN

Sex is hardly ever just about sex.

SHIRLEY MACLAINE

Nobody dies from lack of sex. It's lack of love we die from.

MARGARET ATWOOD

You mustn't force sex to do the work of love or love to do the work of sex.

MARY MCCARTHY

The difference between sex and love is that sex relieves tension and love causes it.

WOODY ALLEN

My hand is not at home in yours.
Your hand is lust—
my hand is longing.

EDITH SÖDERGRAN

Lust is what makes you keep wanting it, even when you have no desire to be with each other. Love is what makes you keep wanting to be with each other, even when you have no desire to do it.

JUDITH VIORST

'Tis better to have loved and lust than never to have loved at all.

CRAIG RICE

Sex and love are like tea and milk. They can be mixed or they can be taken straight. Each has certain distinctive characteristics, but when they are combined they form a unique substance.

JOYCE BROTHERS

Love is music, and sex is only the instrument.

ISABEL ALLENDE

Love lay like a mirage through the golden gates of sex.

DORIS LESSING

Love is the self-delusion we manufacture to justify the trouble we take to have sex.

DAN GREENBURG

There is nothing better for the spirit or body than a love affair. It elevates thoughts and flattens stomachs.

BARBARA HOWAR

Sex is good for about two years, and then you need love.

ZSA ZSA GABOR

Sensuality often grows too fast for love to keep up with. Then love's root remains weak and is easily torn up.

FRIEDRICH NIETZSCHE

Love, I find is like singing. Everybody can do enough to satisfy themselves, though it may not impress the neighbors as being very much.

ZORA NEALE HURSTON

Sex, unlike justice, should not be seen to be done.

EVELYN LAYE

Sex is such a personal thing—why do we insist on sharing it with another person?

JANE WAGNER AND LILY TOMLIN

We are on a sexual binge in this country. . . . One consequence of this binge is that while people now get into bed more readily and a lot more naturally than they once did, what happens there often seems less important.

SHANA ALEXANDER

It *is* something big and cosmic. What else do we have? There's only birth and death and the union of two people—and sex is the only one that happens to us more than once.

KATHLEEN WINSOR

If our sex life were determined by our first youthful experiments, most of the world would be doomed to celibacy. In no area of human experience are human beings more convinced that something better can be had if only they persevere.

P.D. JAMES

As I grew to adolescence, I imagined, from closely observing the boredom and vexations of matrimony, that the act my parents committed and the one I so longed to commit must be two different things.

SHIRLEY ABBOTT

Whoever named it necking was a poor judge of anatomy.

GROUCHO MARX

Whereas a lot of men used to ask for conversation when they really wanted sex, nowadays they often feel obliged to ask for sex even when they really want conversation.

KATHARINE WHITEHORN

I had left home (like all Jewish girls) in order to eat pork and take birth control pills. When I first shared an intimate evening with my husband, I was swept away by the passion (so dormant inside myself) of a long and tortured existence. The physical cravings I had tried so hard to deny, finally and ultimately sated. . . . But enough about the pork.

ROSEANNE BARR

Not only do the young today know more about sex than I did when I was their age, they know more at their age now than I know at my age now.

SAM LEVENSON

Sex is important. Aside from its recreational and entertainment possibilities, it has considerable biological significance. The biological significance was there first; the entertainment value came only recently.

L.L. LARISON CUDMORE

There is nothing that impairs a man's sexual performance quicker than any suggestion that he's not doing it right ("Not *there*, you idiot!").

HELEN LAWRENSON

It was an old quandary for them. He needed sex in order to feel connected to her, and she needed to feel connected to him in order to enjoy sex.

LISA ALTHER

Sex should be a deepening of communication, not a substitute for it.

MARIANNE WILLIAMSON

Hickeys are like PG-13 movies. You think they're pretty hot stuff after being limited to G and PG, but you never bother with them once you're seriously into R.

JUDY MARKEY

It's surely one of the strange phenomena of this decade that the most thoughtful gift you can bring a date is not flowers, chocolates, or ankle-length pearls, but a note from your doctor.

LINDA SUNSHINE

HE HEART

What a mystery the heart is. The mind is simple by comparison.

MARY GORDON

Nobody has ever measured, even the poets, how much a heart can hold.

ZELDA FITZGERALD

In a full heart there is room for everything, and in an empty heart there is room for nothing.

ANTONIO PORCHIA

The heart of another is a dark forest, always, no matter how close it has been to one's own.

WILLA CATHER

It is only with the heart that one can see rightly; what is essential is invisible to the eye.

ANTOINE DE SAINT-EXUPÉRY

The mind divides the world into a million pieces. The heart makes it whole.

STEPHEN AND ONDREA LEVINE

Through love, through friendship, a heart lives more than one life.

ANAÏS NIN

The heart has its reasons, which reason does not know.

PASCAL

All the knowledge I possess everyone else can acquire, but my heart is all my own.

JOHANN WOLFGANG VON GOETHE

The heart likes to tell us what we want to hear.

GOTTHOLD EPHRAIM LESSING

No one dies of a broken heart. Put together and given a reasonable rest cure, an old ticker will get you into almost as much fascinating trouble as a brand new one.

LOUISE BAKER

RELATIONSHIPS

Nobody, but nobody
Can make it out here alone.

MAYA ANGELOU

There is no hope of joy except in human relations.

ANTOINE DE SAINT-EXUPÉRY

Having someone wonder where you are when you
don't come home at night is a very old human need.

MARGARET MEAD

Most real relationships are involuntary.

IRIS MURDOCH

The world has little to bestow
Where two fond hearts in equal love are joined.

ANNA LAETITIA BARBAULD

The most wonderful of all things in life, I believe, is the discovery of another human being with whom one's relationship has a glowing depth, beauty, and joy as the years increase. This inner progressiveness of love between two human beings is a most marvelous thing, it cannot be found by looking for it or by passionately wishing for it. It is a sort of Divine accident.

HUGH WALPOLE

A soul friend is someone with whom we can share our greatest joys and deepest fears, confess our worst sins and most persistent faults, clarify our highest hopes and perhaps most unarticulated dreams.

EDWARD C. SELLNER

Two persons who love each other are in a place
more holy than the interior of a church.

WILLIAM LYON PHELPS

Once the realization is accepted that even between
the *closest* human beings infinite distances continue
to exist, a wonderful living side by side can grow up,
if they succeed in loving the distance between them
which makes it possible for each to see the other
whole against the sky.

RAINER MARIA RILKE

Love that has been given to you is too sacred a thing
to be talked of to anyone . . . except just to the person
who is like part of you and who will feel it as you do.

OLIVE SCHREINER

To be together is for us to be at once as free as in solitude, as gay as in company. We talk, I believe, all day long: to talk to each other is but a more animated and an audible thinking.

CHARLOTTE BRONTË

Two consciousnesses, each dedicated to personal evolution, can provide an extraordinary stimulus and challenge to the other. Then ecstasy can become a way of life.

NATHANIEL BRANDEN

When two people loved each other they worked together always, two against the world, a little company. Joy was shared, trouble was split. You had an ally, somewhere, who was helping.

PAUL GALLICO

Love does not exist, then, until two people can say "we" because that is what they are. This word "we" contains a full and binding pledge: I want to be "with you," and I also wish that you should be "with me." From this moment on I belong to you, and am at your disposal. From now on you will never be alone; even when we are separated, and even when death itself parts us, I shall remain with you.

LADISLAUS BOROS

It takes time and deeds, and this involves trust, it involves making ourselves vulnerable to each other, to strip ourselves naked, to become sitting ducks for each other—and if one of the ducks is shamming, then the sincere duck will pay in pain—but the deceitful duck, I feel, will be the loser.

ELDRIDGE CLEAVER

To love means you also trust.

JOAN BAEZ

How desperately we wish to maintain our trust in those we love! In the face of everything, we try to find reasons to trust. Because losing faith is worse than falling out of love.

SONIA JOHNSON

There is a rule in sailing where the more maneuverable ship should give way to the less maneuverable craft. I think this is sometimes a good rule to follow in human relationships as well.

JOYCE BROTHERS

Intimacy requires courage because risk is inescapable. We cannot know at the outset how the relationships will affect us.

ROLLO MAY

To be emotionally committed to somebody is very difficult, but to be alone is impossible.

STEPHEN SONDHEIM

What greater thing is there for two human souls, than to feel that they are joined for life — to strengthen each other in all labor, to rest on each other in all sorrow, to minister to each other in all pain, to be one with each other in silent unspeakable memories at the moment of the last parting?

GEORGE ELIOT

Tenderness is greater proof of love than the most passionate of vows.

MARLENE DIETRICH

The perfect relationship does not come from finding the "perfect person," but from finding a person perfect for you.

STEPHEN AND ONDREA LEVINE

The gift that is given in love is ultimately always the giver himself. All the other gifts which may be received in love are shot through with the splendor of this self-giving. The real giving in love takes place, not on the lowly level of what I have and what I possess, but on the exalted plane of what I am.

LADISLAUS BOROS

When a love relationship is at its height there is no room left for any interest in the environment; a pair of lovers are sufficient to themselves.

SIGMUND FREUD

One hardly dares to say that love is the core of the relationship, though love is sought for and created in relationship; love is rather the marvel when it is there, but it is not always there, and to know another and to be known by another—that is everything.

FLORIDA SCOTT-MAXWELL

Intimate relationships cannot substitute for a life plan. But to have any meaning or viability at all, a life plan must include intimate relationships.

HARRIET LERNER

You can't have relationships with other people until you give birth to yourself.

SONIA SANCHEZ

Union is only possible to those who are units. To be fit for relations in time, souls, whether of man or woman, must be able to do without them in the spirit.

MARGARET FULLER

The emotion, the ecstasy of love, we all want, but God spare us the responsibility.

JESSAMYN WEST

If one really does try to find out why it is that people don't leave each other, one discovers a mystery. It is because they can't; they are bound. And nobody on earth knows what are the bonds that bind them except those two.

KATHERINE MANSFIELD

Love, which is a madness, and a scourge, and a fever, and a delusion, and a snare, is also a mystery, and very imperfectly understood by everyone except the individual sufferer who writhes under its tortures.

MARY ELIZABETH BRADDON

Equality is always the strongest bond of love.

GOTTHOLD EPHRAIM LESSING

Compassion is the most necessary ingredient in all relationships. Everything depends on it.

JANE STANTON HITCHCOCK

Him that I love, I wish to be
Free—
Even from me.

ANNE MORROW LINDBERGH

Give your hearts, but not into each other's keeping. For only the hand of Life can contain your hearts. And stand together yet not too near together: For the pillars of the temple stand apart, And the oak tree and the cypress grow not in each other's shadow.

KAHLIL GIBRAN

Their bodies were so close together that there was no room for real affection.

STANISLAW J. LEC

She felt ill-suited to the mystery of being in a relationship. Relationship—that silk purse turned sow's ear. . . . Ensnared in a relentless beam of scrutiny, the only motion you could achieve was coming up short.

CARRIE FISHER

Can I ever know you
Or you know me?

SARA TEASDALE

Let there be spaces in your togetherness,
And let the winds of the heavens dance between you.
Love one another, but make not a bond of love. . . .
Fill each other's cup but drink not from one cup.

KAHLIL GIBRAN

A relationship isn't meant to be an insurance policy,
a life preserver or a security blanket.

DIANE CROWLEY

What if you leave and never return,
and worse, what if you return and never leave.
I fear being alone, but what if I tell you that
even more I fear never being alone.

CAROL CONNOLLY

No partner in a love relationship (whether homo- or
heterosexual) should feel that he has to give up an
essential part of himself to make it viable.

MAY SARTON

Let me not to the marriage of true minds
Admit impediments. Love is not love
Which alters when it alteration finds.

SHAKESPEARE

What is missing in him is probably necessary for what is missing in you. Let us not to the marriage of true impediments admit minds.

JEAN KERR

We love best those who are, or act for us, a self we do not wish to be or act out.

ANAÏS NIN

It's only in silence that you can judge of your relationship to a person.

DOROTHY M. RICHARDSON

In love, nothing is as eloquent as mutual silence.

MICHELE MORGAN

It is explained that all relationships require a little give and take. This is untrue. Any partnership demands that we give and give and give and at the last, as we flop into our graves exhausted, we are told that we didn't give enough.

QUENTIN CRISP

There is probably nothing like living together for blinding people to each other.

IVY COMPTON-BURNETT

"Love is blind." But it may be the other way around. Love allows a person to see the true angelic nature of another person, the halo, the aureole of divinity.

THOMAS MOORE

Love is blind: that is why it always proceeds by the sense of touch.

ANONYMOUS

I think true love is never blind,
But rather brings an added light;
An inner vision quick to find
The beauties hid from common sight.

PHOEBE CARY

Love is the greatest beautifier in the universe.

MAY CHRISTIE

It is better to know as little as possible of the defects
of the person with whom you are to pass your life.

JANE AUSTEN

This was life, that two people, no matter how care-
fully chosen, could not be everything to each other.

DORIS LESSING

Cupid's arrows rarely strike two people with the same definition of cleanliness.

MARGO KAUFMAN

No two people have the same ideas about how often to take out the trash, how often to dry-clean the slip-covers, how many fingerprints on a windowpane definitely constitute "filth."

STEPHANIE BRUSH

During a quarrel, to have said too little may be mended; to have said too much, not always.

MINNA THOMAS ANTRIM

Bad quarrels come when two people are wrong. Worse quarrels come when two people are right.

BETTY SMITH

They had quarreled about this single, solitary sore point: their life.

ANNIE DILLARD

They buried the hatchet, but in a shallow, well-marked grave.

DOROTHY WALWORTH

Rarely an hour passed that they didn't argue about something. They had lived together for so many years that they mistook their arguments for conversations.

MARJORIE KELLOGG

When one person's mad and the other isn't, the mad one always wins.

MARY O'HARA

Never go to bed mad—stay up and fight.

PHYLLIS DILLER

A happy home is one in which each spouse grants the possibility that the other may be right, though neither believes it.

DON FRASER

Manners are not just something to show off to the outside world. If you offend the head waiter, you can always go to another restaurant. If you offend the person you live with, it's very cumbersome to switch to a different family.

JUDITH MARTIN

Sharing is sometimes more demanding than giving.

MARY CATHERINE BATESON

What kind of word is "commitment," anyway? "He was *committed* to an institution for the criminally insane." "She was *committed* to the federal penitentiary because she had *committed* manslaughter." Right away you know "commitment" is not a fun word. Why would men and women want to *commit* themselves to anything? And what's more, why should they have to?

DAN GREENBURG AND SUZANNE O'MALLEY

A therapist lays bare the "inner workings" of your relationship. Who wields the power? Who is the "Parent"? Who is the "Fascist"? Who is the "Big Cheese"? Who is the "Cottage Cheese"? Who is the "Little Tomato"?

STEPHANIE BRUSH

"If only you were you and yet not you!"
There is no peace with you
Nor ever any rest!

JESSIE REDMOND FAUSET

I can't live either without you or with you.

OVID

Ah, how much I like you, how well we get on,
when you're asleep and I'm awake.

COLETTE

I love you no matter what you do, but do you have
to do so much of it?

JEAN ILLSLEY CLARKE

ARRIAGE

If kissing and being engaged were this inflammatory, marriage must burn clear to the bone. I wondered how flesh and blood could endure the ecstasy. How did married couples manage to look so calm and unexcited?

JESSAMYN WEST

Marriage is the most delightful of the impermanencies of life.

ANTHONY GILBERT

Nothing in life is as good as the marriage of true minds between man and woman. As good? It is life itself.

PEARL S. BUCK

A happy marriage is still the greatest treasure within the gift of fortune.

EDEN PHILLPOTTS

A happy marriage is a long conversation that always seems too short.

ANDRÉ MAUROIS

In a happy marriage there is a continuous dense magnetic sense of communication.

IRIS MURDOCH

Maybe being married is talking to oneself with one's other self listening.

RUTH RENDELL

Often the difference between a successful marriage and a mediocre one consists of leaving about three or four things a day unsaid.

HARLAN MILLER

A happy marriage is the union of two forgivers.

RUTH BELL GRAHAM

Sexiness wears thin after a while and beauty fades, but to be married to a man who makes you laugh every day, ah, now that's a real treat!

JOANNE WOODWARD

The real marriage of true minds is for any two people to possess a sense of humor or irony pitched in exactly the same key, so that their joint glances at any subject cross like interarching searchlights.

EDITH WHARTON

There is in marriage an energy and impulse of joy that lasts as long as life and that survives all sorts of suffering and distress and weariness. The triumph of marriage over all its antagonists is almost inexplicable.

JAMES DOUGLAS

Those who have made unhappy marriages walk on stilts, while the happy ones are on a level with the crowd. No one sees 'em!

JOHN OLIVER HOBBES

Marriage is like twirling a baton, turning a handspring or eating with chopsticks; it looks so easy until you try it.

HELEN ROWLAND

People are still marrying for better or for worse, for richer or for poorer, but not for long.

SAM LEVENSON

There's only one way to make a happy marriage, and most husbands and wives would like to know what it is.

ANONYMOUS

Sometimes it was worth all the disadvantages of marriage just to have that: one friend in an indifferent world.

ERICA JONG

Marriage resembles a pair of shears, so joined that they cannot be separated; often moving in opposite directions, yet always punishing anyone who comes between them.

SYDNEY SMITH

One advantage of marriage, it seems to me, is that when you fall out of love with him, or he falls out of love with you, it keeps you together until you maybe fall in again.

JUDITH VIORST

There are two marriages . . . in every marital union, his and hers.

JESSIE BERNARD

Marriage often unites for life two people who scarcely know each other.

HONORÉ DE BALZAC

Marriage has teeth, and him bite very hot.

JAMAICAN PROVERB

When two people are under the influence of the most violent, most insane, most delusive, and most transient of passions, they are required to swear that they will remain in that excited, abnormal, and exhausting condition continuously until death do them part.

GEORGE BERNARD SHAW

As a general thing, people marry most happily with their own kind. The trouble lies in the fact that people usually marry at an age when they do not really know what their own kind is.

ROBERTSON DAVIES

If you made a list of the reasons why any couple got married, and another list of the reasons for their divorce, you'd have a hell of a lot of overlapping.

MIGNON MCLAUGHLIN

It was only long after the ceremony
That we learned
Why we got married
In the first place.

LOIS WYSE

Chains do not hold a marriage together. It is
threads, hundreds of tiny threads, which sew people
together through the years. That's what makes a
marriage last more than passion or sex.

SIMONE SIGNORET

Nearly all marriages, even happy ones, are mistakes;
in the sense that almost certainly (in a more perfect
world, or even with a little more care in this very
imperfect one) both partners might have found
more suitable mates. But the real soul-mate is the
one you are actually married to.

J.R.R. TOLKEIN

The bonds of matrimony are like any other bonds—they mature slowly.

PETER DE VRIES

Take each other for better or worse but not for granted.

ARLENE DAHL

Each coming together of man and wife, even if they have been mated for many years, should be a fresh adventure; each winning should necessitate a fresh wooing.

MARIE STOPES

True intimacy is frightening, and I was well into my marriage before I realized that I either had to seek it or live a lie. Intimacy is what makes a marriage, not a ceremony, not a piece of paper from the state.

KATHLEEN NORRIS

The people who enjoy marriage are those who first have learned to live life itself. You can't create intimacy without identity.

RICHARD ROHR

Marriage is a thing you've got to give your whole mind to.

HENRIK IBSEN

There is no more lovely, friendly, and charming relationship, communion, or company than a good marriage.

MARTIN LUTHER

I do not . . . pretend to have discovered that life has anything more to be desired than a prudent and virtuous marriage.

SAMUEL JOHNSON

Ay, marriage is the life-long miracle,
The self-begetting wonder, daily fresh.

CHARLES KINGSLEY

Some pray to marry the man they love,
My prayer will somewhat vary:
I humbly pray to Heaven above
That I love the man I marry.

ROSE PASTOR STOKES

Keep your eyes wide open before marriage, half
shut afterwards.

BENJAMIN FRANKLIN

The people people have for friends
Your common sense appall,
But the people people marry
Are the queerest folk of all.

CHARLOTTE PERKINS GILMAN

There is one thing I can't get in my head—
Why *do* people marry the people they wed?

CAROLYN WELLS

The men that women marry,
And why they marry them, will always be
A marvel and a mystery to the world.

HENRY WADSWORTH LONGFELLOW

Marriage is popular because it combines the maximum of temptation with the maximum of opportunity.

GEORGE BERNARD SHAW

Marriage should be a duet—when one sings, the other claps.

JOE MURRAY

It is easier to be a lover than a husband for the simple reason that it is more difficult to be witty every day than to say pretty things from time to time.

HONORÉ DE BALZAC

A lover may be a shadowy creature, but husbands are made of flesh and blood.

AMY LEVY

If any man truly believes that he is the boss of his house, then let him do this: pick up the phone, call a wallpaper store, order new wallpaper for one of the rooms in his house, and then put it on. He would have a longer life expectancy sprinkling arsenic on his eggs. Any husband who buys wallpaper, drapes, or even a prayer rug on his own is auditioning for the Bureau of Missing Persons.

BILL COSBY

It is a matter of life and death for married people to interrupt each other's stories; for if they did not, they would burst.

LOGAN PEARSALL SMITH

I have always believed that the key to a happy marriage was the ability to say with a straight face, "Why, I don't know what you're worrying about. I thought you were very funny last night and I'm sure everybody else did, too."

JUDITH MARTIN

A man loves a woman so much, he asks her to marry—to change her name, quit her job, have and raise his babies, be home when he gets there, move where his job is. You can hardly imagine what he might ask if he didn't love her.

GABRIELLE BURTON

If it hadn't been for my wife, I couldn't have stood married life.

DON HEROLD

You know that the urge for revenge is a fact of marital life.

JANE SMILEY

The best part of married life is the fights. The rest is merely so-so.

THORNTON WILDER

If it weren't for marriage, men and women would have to fight with total strangers.

ANONYMOUS

A married couple are well suited when both partners usually feel the need for a quarrel at the same time.

JEAN ROSTAND

Marriage is an alliance entered into by a man who can't sleep with the window shut, and a woman who can't sleep with the window open.

GEORGE BERNARD SHAW

Molehills *are* mountains when you are first married.

KATHLEEN NORRIS

We would have broken up except for the children. Who were the children? Well, she and I were.

MORT SAHL

In every marriage there are the elements of success, and in every one the makings of a perfectly justifiable divorce.

KATHLEEN NORRIS

A successful marriage requires falling in love many times, always with the same person.

MIGNON MCLAUGHLIN

It takes a long time to be really married. One marries many times at many levels within a marriage. If you have more marriages than you have divorces within the marriage, you're lucky and you stick it out.

RUBY DEE

There are no successful marriages. There are only those that are succeeding—or failing.

WELLS GOODRICH

I suspect that in every good marriage there are times when love seems to be over.

MADELEINE L'ENGLE

There are two tests in a happy marriage—riches and poverty.

ANONYMOUS

Any marriage worth the name is no better than a series of beginnings—many of them abortive.

STORM JAMESON

In the true marriage relation, the independence of the husband and wife is equal, the dependence mutual and their obligations reciprocal.

LUCRETIA MOTT

The sum which two married people owe to one another defies calculation. It is an infinite debt, which can only be discharged through all eternity.

JOHANN WOLFGANG VON GOETHE

Success in marriage is much more than a matter of finding the right person; it is also a matter of *being* the right person.

LELAND FOSTER WOOD

Marriage is our last, best chance to grow up.

JOSEPH BARTH

Marriage . . . hath in it less of beauty, but more of safety, than the single life; it hath more care, but less danger; it is more merry, and more sad; it is fuller of sorrows, and fuller of joys; it lies under more burdens, but is supported by all the strengths of love and charity, and those burdens are delightful.

JEREMY TAYLOR

No human being can destroy the structure of a marriage except the two who made it. It is the one human edifice that is impregnable except from within.

GWEN BRISTOW

I used to believe that marriage would diminish me, reduce my options. That you had to be someone less to live with someone else when, of course, you have to be someone more.

CANDICE BERGEN

If the right man does not come along, there are
many fates far worse. One is to have the wrong man
come along.

LETITIA BALDRIGE

Marriage is like a cage: one sees the birds outside
desperate to get in, and those inside equally desperate to get out.

MICHEL EYQUEM DE MONTAIGNE

Love pleases more than marriage, for the reason that
romance is more interesting than history.

SÉBASTIEN NICOLAS CHAMFORT

The deep, deep peace of the double-bed after the
hurly-burly of the chaise longue.

MRS. PATRICK CAMPBELL

It is true that I never should have married, but I didn't want to live without a man. Brought up to respect the conventions, love had to end in marriage. I'm afraid it did.

BETTE DAVIS

Marriage is a great strain upon love.

MYRTLE REED

Marriage wrecks any decent relationship.

SUSAN STRAIGHT

The reason that husbands and wives do not understand each other is because they belong to different sexes.

DOROTHY DIX

If men and wimmen think they are marryin' angels, they'll find out they'll have to settle down and keep house with human critters. I never see a year yet, that didn't have more or less winter in it.

JOSIAH ALLEN'S WIFE

Marriage is an edifice that must be rebuilt every day.

ANDRÉ MAUROIS

Marriage isn't a 50-50 proposition very often. It's more like 100-0 one moment and 0-100 the next.

BILLIE JEAN KING

Whoever thinks marriage is a fifty-fifty proposition doesn't know the half of it.

FRANKLIN P. JONES

A man is very revealed by his wife, just as a woman is revealed by her husband. People never marry beneath or above themselves, I assure you.

CAROL MATTHAU

Love is a beautiful story and marriage is the talkie version of it.

MARTHA LUPTON

There's nothing wrong with marriage; it's just the living together afterward that's murder.

SAM LEVENSON

Love is blind and marriage is an eye doctor.

MARTHA LUPTON

Marriage enables a husband to find out what kind of husband his wife would have preferred.

ANONYMOUS

The trend indicates that marrying the one you love is much easier than loving the one you married, and that constancy in marriage is much harder than constantly getting married.

SAM LEVENSON

A girl must marry for love, and keep on marrying until she finds it.

ZSA ZSA GABOR

Marriage is too interesting an experiment to be tried only once or twice.

EVA GABOR

Marriage is like a merry-go-round. I keep getting on different horses, but it's the same ride.

ALTA

I have had a couple of marriages, but like every other woman I had a perfect right to them.

MARIE DRESSLER

It is ridiculous to think you can spend your entire life with just one person. Three is about the right number. Yes, I imagine three husbands would do it.

CLARE BOOTHE LUCE

I've married a few people I shouldn't have, but haven't we all?

MAMIE VAN DOREN

It is as absurd to pretend that one cannot love the same woman always, as to pretend that a good artist needs several violins to execute a piece of music.

HONORÉ DE BALZAC

Marriage is a great institution, but I'm not ready for an institution yet.

MAE WEST

 BSENCE

In the arithmetic of love, one plus one equals everything, and two minus one equals nothing.

MIGNON MCLAUGHLIN

When you're away i feel like
i'm only wearing one shoe.

ALTA

Where you used to be, there is a hole in the world,
which I find myself constantly walking around in
the day-time, and falling into at night. I miss you
like hell.

EDNA ST. VINCENT MILLAY

Absence on Love effects the same
As winds oppos'd to fire
Extinguishes a feeble Flame
And blows a great one higher.

ANNE FINCH

Absence diminishes mediocre passions and increases great ones, as the wind blows out candles and fans fire.

FRANÇOIS DE LA ROCHEFOUCAULD

Absence in love is like water upon fire, a little quickens, but much extinguishes it.

HANNAH MORE

It is only love that has already fallen sick that is killed by absence.

DIANE DE POITIERS

I am perfectly sad at parting from you. I could better have the earth taken away from under my feet, than the thought of you from my mind.

HENRY DAVID THOREAU

How long time is when one is sad! Is it three years
or three days since you went away. . . ?

EUGÉNIE DE GUÉRIN

I do not love thee!—no! I do not love thee!
And yet when thou art absent I am sad.

CAROLINE E. S. NORTON

Absence makes the heart grow fonder.

THOMAS HAYNES BAYLY

Absence makes the heart grow fonder,
And presents make it fonder still.

ROSE HENNIKER HEATON

WOMEN AND MEN

Men and women belong to different species and communication between them is a science still in its infancy.

BILL COSBY

I believe in the difference between men and women. In fact, I embrace the difference.

ELIZABETH TAYLOR

Seems to me the basic conflict between men and women, sexually, is that men are like firemen. To us, sex is an emergency, and no matter what we're doing we can be ready in two minutes. Women, on the other hand, are like fire. They're very exciting, but the conditions have to be exactly right for it to occur.

JERRY SEINFELD

Sometimes I wonder if men and women really suit each other. Perhaps they should live next-door and just visit now and then.

KATHARINE HEPBURN

Man and woman are two locked caskets, of which each contains the key to the other.

ISAK DINESEN

The difference between man's love and woman's is she loves with all her heart and soul; he, with all his mind and body.

MINNA THOMAS ANTRIM

Love comes to man through his senses—to woman through her imagination.

JOHN OLIVER HOBBES

A man falls in love through his eyes, a woman through her imagination, and then they both speak of it as an affair of "the heart."

HELEN ROWLAND

A man when he is making up to anybody can be cordial and gallant and full of little attentions and altogether charming. But when a man is really in love he can't help looking like a sheep.

AGATHA CHRISTIE

Plenty of guys are good at sex, but conversation, now there's an art.

LINDA BARNES

A man'll seem like a person to a woman, year in, year out. She'll put up and she'll put up. Then one day he'll do something maybe no worse than what he's been a-doing all his life. She'll look at him. And without no warning he'll look like a varmint.

MARJORIE KINNAN RAWLINGS

She'll throw herself at his head until he loses consciousness, and then she'll marry him.

RUTH SAWYER

Let this serve as an axiom to every lover: A woman who refuses lunch refuses everything.

ENID BAGNOLD

No matter how happily a woman may be married, it always pleases her to discover that there is a nice man who wishes that she were not.

H.L. MENCKEN

 **IRST LOVES**

I'm glad it cannot happen twice, the fever of first love.

DAPHNE DU MAURIER

It was first love. There's no love like that. I don't wish it on a soul. I don't hate anyone enough.

CAROL MATTHAU

First love is an astounding experience and if the object happens to be totally unworthy and the love not really love at all, it makes little difference to the intensity or the pain.

ANGELA THIRKELL

Love is the last and most serious of the diseases of childhood.

ANONYMOUS

Many of us are done with adolescence before we are done with adolescent love.

JUDITH VIORST

When first we fall in love, we feel that we know all there is to know about life, and perhaps we are right.

MIGNON MCLAUGHLIN

Reason to the lovesick was fire to the feverish. It sent them clean out of their minds.

JESSAMYN WEST

The mark of a true crush . . . is that you fall in love first and grope for reasons afterward.

SHANA ALEXANDER

Infatuation is one of those slightly comic illnesses which are at once so undignified and so painful that a nice-minded world does its best to ignore their existence altogether, referring to them only under provocation and then with apology, but, like its more material brother, this boil on the neck of the spirit can hardly be forgotten either by the sufferer or anyone else in his vicinity. The malady is ludicrous, sad, excruciating and, above all, instantly diagnosable.

MARGERY ALLINGHAM

Infatuation is when you think that he's as sexy as Robert Redford, as smart as Henry Kissinger, as noble as Ralph Nader, as funny as Woody Allen and as athletic as Jimmy Connors. Love is when you realize that he's as sexy as Woody Allen, as smart as Jimmy Connors, as funny as Ralph Nader, as athletic as Henry Kissinger and nothing like Robert Redford— but you'll take him anyway.

JUDITH VIORST

If you love the wrong people it's still love, isn't it, no matter what kind of love.

RUMER GODDEN

In real love you want the other person's good. In romantic love you want the other person.

MARGARET ANDERSON

No one can understand love who has not experienced infatuation. And no one can understand infatuation, no matter how many times he has experienced it.

MIGNON MCLAUGHLIN

But there's nothing half so sweet in life
As love's young dream.

THOMAS MOORE

Young Love may go,
For aught I care,
To Jericho!

THOMAS MOORE

$\mathcal{L}$ATER LOVES

It's never too late to have a fling,
For Autumn is just as nice as Spring,
And it's never too late to fall in love.

SANDY WILSON

The greatest love is that we know,
When life is just an afterglow.

GEORGIA DOUGLAS JOHNSON

Dawn love is silver,
Wait for the west:
Old love is gold love—
Old love is best.

KATHARINE LEE BATES

Love is like the measles. The older you get it, the worse the attack.

MARY ROBERTS RINEHART

Age doesn't protect you from love. But love, to some extent, protects you from age.

JEANNE MOREAU

Those who love deeply never grow old; they may die of old age, but they die young.

ARTHUR WING PINERO

A long-term romance is like a rose bush. In any given season, a blossom might fall off. But if the plant is well nourished, then the season will come around again, and new blossoms appear.

MARIANNE WILLIAMSON

The memories of long love gather like drifting snow, poignant as the mandarin ducks who float side by side in sleep.

LADY MURASAKI

Love seems the swiftest, but it is the slowest of all growths. No man or woman really knows what perfect love is until they have been married a quarter of a century.

MARK TWAIN

We are not the same persons this year as last; nor are those we love. It is a happy chance if we, changing, continue to love a changed person.

W. SOMERSET MAUGHAM

The concept of two people living together for twenty-five years without having a cross word suggests a lack of spirit only to be admired in sheep.

A.P. HERBERT

Grow old along with me!
The best is yet to be,
The last of life, for which the first was made.

ROBERT BROWNING

Habit, of which passion must be wary, may all the same be the sweetest part of love.

ELIZABETH BOWEN

In love, gallantry is necessary. Even when the first wild desire is gone, especially then, there is an inherent need for good manners and consideration, for the putting forth of effort. Two courteous and civilized human beings out of the loneliness of their souls owe that to each other.

ILKA CHASE

If the second marriage really succeeds, the first one didn't really fail.

MIGNON MCLAUGHLIN

Love is what you have been through with someone.

REBECCA LEVENSON

When one has once had the good luck to love intensely, life is spent in trying to recapture that ardor and that illumination.

ALBERT CAMUS

We always believe our first love is our last, and our last love our first.

GEORGE WHYTE-MELVILLE

ROBABLY NOT LOVE

After all, my erstwhile dear,
My no longer cherished,
Need we say it was not love,
Just because it perished?

EDNA ST. VINCENT MILLAY

How do you know that love is gone? If you said you would be there at seven, you get there by nine and he or she has not called the police yet—it's gone.

MARLENE DIETRICH

When we discuss those we love with those who do not love them, the end of love is near.

MIGNON MCLAUGHLIN

Take me or leave me; or, as is the usual order of things, both.

DOROTHY PARKER

It destroys one's nerves to be amiable every day to the same human being.

BENJAMIN DISRAELI

I am not a cold woman, Henry,
But I do not feel for you,
What I feel for the elephants and the miasmas
And the general view.

STEVIE SMITH

The tragedy of love is indifference.

W. SOMERSET MAUGHAM

The end
of passion
may refashion
a friend.

MONA VAN DUYN

We had a lot in common, I loved him and he loved him.

SHELLEY WINTERS

I just broke up with someone after three years. It was a love-hate thing. We both loved him and hated me.

CAROL SISKIND

Many a happy marriage is due to the fact that they both are in love with the same woman.

ANONYMOUS

Marriage is like paying an endless visit in your worst clothes.

J.B. PRIESTLEY

Love, shmove. I love blintzes; did I marry one?

PAPA LEVENSON

We cannot really love anybody with whom we never laugh.

AGNES REPPLIER

Grumbling is the death of love.

MARLENE DIETRICH

I don't understand you. Monday you liked fried herring, Tuesday you liked fried herring, Wednesday you liked fried herring, now all of a sudden Thursday you don't like fried herring!

SAM LEVENSON

Faults are thick where love is thin.

CHRISTOPHER HARVEY

Free love is priced right.

EDWARD ABBEY

Free love is too expensive.

BERNADETTE DEVLIN

In their first passion women love their lovers, in all the others they love love.

FRANÇOIS DE LA ROCHEFOUCAULD

'Tis said, woman loves not her lover
So much as she loves his love of her;
Then loves she her lover
For love of her lover,
Or love of her love of her lover?

CAROLYN WELLS

The only difference between a caprice and a life-long passion is that the caprice lasts a little longer.

OSCAR WILDE

Romance, like a ghost, eludes touching. It is always where you were, not where you are.

GEORGE W. CURTIS

All discarded lovers should be given a second chance, but with somebody else.

MAE WEST

The mind has a thousand eyes,
And the heart but one;
Yet the light of a whole life dies
When love is done.

FRANCIS WILLIAM BOURDILLION

Where there is no longer love, there is no longer anything.

GEORGE SAND